T0146643

Financial Competency...
A Roadmap to Financial Well Being

Financial Competency...
A Roadmap to Financial Well Being

Create The Life You Want to Live!!

Leslie D. Reed
with Ronald L. Robinson

authorHOUSE

AuthorHouse™
1663 Liberty Drive
Bloomington, IN 47403
www.authorhouse.com
Phone: 1 (800) 839-8640

Published by AuthorHouse   03/17/2016

ISBN: 978-1-5049-4843-2 (sc)
ISBN: 978-1-5049-4842-5 (e)

Library of Congress Control Number: 2015916072

Print information available on the last page.

Roadmap

UNIT 1:

TITLE: EMPLOYEE LITERACY 1

GOAL: "BECOMING A VALUED EMPLOYEE"

1. Employee Literacy: 2
2. What Does Employment Mean? 2
3. Assessing Abilities: Education, Skills, Aptitudes (Knowing Yourself... Making Yourself The Best You Can Be) 2
4. Getting A Job (This Is Where The Work Begins) 3
5. Keeping A Job & Your Work Ethic (Workplace Primer) 7
6. Becoming A Valued Employee….Growing As An Employee 11
7. Translating Employee Literacy Into Greater Productivity & Profit 12
8. Payoff: 14

UNIT 2:

TITLE: "DYNAMICS OF MONEY & MONEY MANAGEMENT" 15

GOAL: TO BETTER BUDGET, MAINTAIN A GOOD BANKING RELATIONSHIP, ESTABLISH AND MAINTAIN A GOOD CREDIT RATING, PROTECT, SAVE AND MAKE OUR MONEY GROW

9. Dynamics Of Money & Money Management: 16
10. Budgeting 17
11. Banking Relationship (Establishing & Maintaining A Checking Account) 18
12. Credit Management: 22
13. Saving: 24
14. Life Insurance Protection & Retirement Savings 28
15. Wealth Transfer 32
16. Benefits Of Wealth Transfer Planning With Life Insurance 33
17. Tax Refunds (Return) Using It Effectively 34

UNIT 3:

TITLE: EMPLOYER LITERACY 37

GOAL: UNLOCKING THE POTENTIAL, POWER AND PRODUCTIVITY OF EMPLOYEES BY UNDERSTANDING THE CONCEPT OF EMPLOYMENT BY LOOKING AT THE NEEDS & WANTS OF AN EMPLOYER

18. Definition of Employer Literacy 37
19. How Does A Business Continue To Operate? 38
20. What Employers Need & Want...38
21. Discussion: Exercise to get the needed "buy in" from the employee 39

UNIT 4:

TITLE: ENTREPRENUER COMPETENCY 41

GOAL "TO BETTER UNDERSTAND THE AMERICAN SYSTEM OF FREE ENTERPRISE. TO LEARN THE STEPS NECESSARY TO: ESTABLISH AND CREATE A BUSINESS THAT CAN SURVIVE AND PROSPER IN THE MARKETPLACE." (RIM GROUP, 2013)

22. Defining entrepreneurship literacy 41
23. Identifying And Starting A Business Venture...42
24. Steps in starting a business..43
25. Acquirng & Organizing The Required Resources 44
26. Financial Resources: 45
27. Other Sources Of Raising Capital: 47
28. Risks And Rewards: 48

Why I Wrote The Book

The term **"FINANCIAL LITERACY"** is being used so often the actual meaning is not resonating with people in a way that can change their lives. We believe that the true meaning has to be practical and useful in a way that can help people develop the knowledge & skills to: take care of their children, pay bills without stress, or just be able to enjoy some of life's pleasures. Quite simply, people want to function normally in our American way of life. Financial Literacy should be the formula for successful living. It is not just budgets or finance, it is being able to understand and utilize an effective discipline, with the end result being; a better lifestyle and peace of mind. Here is our working definition of financial literacy:

"KNOWLEDGE OF THE LIFE & MONEY SKILLS NECESSARY TO OPERATE YOUR FINANCES, INCLUDING; EMPLOYMENT, SPENDING & SAVINGS HABITS, HOW MONEY GROWS, HOW YOU GROW IN THE EMPLOYMENT ENVIRONMENT, AND ULTIMATELY HOW TO MAKE THESE DECISIONS LAST THROUGH GENERATIONS" (RIM Group 2013)

This book wants to give the participant a practical, fundamentally based methodology in their approach to "Financial Literacy". We will approach the matter of financial literacy from several aspects, attempting to enlarge the participant's current perspective. This course/seminar has been developed by businessmen who know what it takes to be financially successful and are in the workplace daily. We want to impart skills that will enable you to truly know and understand your finances; but more importantly give you the tools to enable you to operate in a way that can affect your day to day life and lifestyle. We will approach this from several perspectives.

We will be guided by two central premises:

1. **YOU NEED TO HAVE A WAY TO MAKE MONEY. YOU CAN'T HAVE FINANCIAL LITERACY WITHOUT MONEY!** In most cases it is getting and keeping a job. In other situations it may be creating a money making entity (self employment, owning a company). In either case there are guidelines/rules that you need to know in order to "play the game."

2. **YOUR MONEY NEEDS TO BE: PROPERLY MANAGED and GROWING... YOUR MONEY NEEDS TO CREATE A LEGACY FOR YOUR FAMILY!** You should make,

manage, and grow money. If this happens you will have money to pass on to the next generation. These key premises are interconnected. When we understand that they work together, we have the necessary pieces to the puzzle. We want to help you break the cycle of the **"PAYCHECK TO PAYCHECK MENTALITY"**.

Acknowledgements

Thank you God…you are awesome!!! I thank you for Jesus. I thank my mother Chevis Elaine Reed, who always told me that "I know so I must do"…..This book is dedicated to Men who want to be good providers and fathers. To Women who continue to be extraordinary Mothers loving and taking care of our children.

To my girls Amanda and Logen I admire your tenacity, understanding and growing wisdom…. You are my pride!!!

Thank You Christian Theological Seminary, for the opportunity to explore and study all things spiritual.

To the men of Degroupe…."it is this thing among us"

To my very special Coach H. Chatmon…..Peace & Love!!

Golden Ghetto U.S…..a true American aesthetic

To the Sons of the American Revolution…you set the blueprint for the "American Way". Capitalism, love it or hate it…it's still the best game in the world.

Special thanks to Eboni Kelly for her special touches and Dr. Maxine L. Bryant for her valuable editing contribution.

To anybody that this book helps…You are my muse.

Back cover picture of Leslie D. Reed courtesy Cliff Robinson Scoop Media Group

Preface

Why be Financially Competent? ….Why have wealth?

Certainly for the things that money can buy….definitely for peace of mind. I would like to suggest that the best expression of our wealth is how it can affect and change the lives of our families, those we love, and the world we live in. You ever seen a sunset? It's more magnificentwhen it is shared. Go on a nice vacation? It's better with the one you love by your side. Ever have to say no to your children? Saying yes is better, and the world needs more yes's. I am talking to you about a motivation to have financial well being beyond money…sure it's the vacation, or a sunset, and for sure it is peace of mind. Beyond these things we have to believe that we are entitled to prosper and more importantly, we are commanded to use that prosperity for the good of others.

I found this quote and it sums up well what I am trying to express:

> **"If you want to be rich, be generous. If you want to make friends, be friendly. If you want to be heard, listen. If you want to be understood by others, take the time to truly understand them. If you want to live an interesting life, be interested in the happenings around you".**

Melchor Lim quotes

I conclude by saying that we should have wealth. For all of the right reasons which includes enjoying the fruits of our wealth (nice things that money can buy, even the status that being wealthy brings…if that gives you joy, go for it). I am also lining up with the import of the quote which is generosity…caring…and living the life that we deserve. It is in living and reflecting in our lives' this way that we have true wealth. This is my desire for you….

HAVE WEALTH!!!

(Excerpt from Scoop Magazine Column Money Talk, June 2015 titled, "Why Have Wealth by Leslie D. Reed)

This Book will:

1. Look at the dynamic of employment, from being hired, getting and keeping a job. How do we operate in the workplace? How does this translate into greater productivity, and ultimately profitability for the company? (Employee Literacy)

2. Look at the dynamic of having money and the ability to budget, protect, save and make your money grow. Discuss the need to have a banking relationship and good credit.

3. Look at the dynamic of employment from an employer's perspective. (Employer Literacy)

4. Look at the dynamic of self employment, entrepreneurship, legal obstacles, and the American Dream. (Entrepreneur Literacy)

The true payoff & payback:

- We want to help you break the cycle of the **"PAYCHECK TO PAYCHECK MENTALITY." WE WANT TO HELP YOU CREATE LASTING FINANCIAL PROSPERITY FOR YOUR FAMILY.....THIS LEADS TO GENERATIONAL WEALTH WHICH IS GOOD FOR YOUR FAMILY & OUR SOCIETY...IT IS THE WIN/WIN!!**

AUTHORS NOTE:

In writing this book and considering the audience who might read it I took into consideration, 1. People who would read the book for their own personal information and knowledge and 2. People who might instruct, teach and conduct seminars/courses using the material I have written about. With these considerations in mind the book uses phrases that address both these audiences. As a result, I will reference participants, course/seminar as well as points in the book where a discussion may help the learning experience or a handout might be used to further enhance understanding of a key point. I have in certain places in the book inserted the term commentary as well to broaden and further expound on key thoughts and ideas that I feel will be even more helpful and useful in reading this book.

Introduction

COMPETENCE OR COMPETENCY: A WORKING DEFINITION.....

Some scholars see "competence" as a combination of practical and theoretical knowledge, cognitive skills, behavior and values used to improve performance; or as the state or quality of being adequately or well qualified, having the ability to perform a specific role. For instance, life management competency might include systems thinking and emotional intelligence, and skills in influence and negotiation.

Competency is also used as a more general description of the requirements of human beings in organizations and communities.

Competency is sometimes thought of as being shown in action in a situation and context that might be different the next time a person has to act. In emergencies, competent people may react to a situation following behaviors they have previously found to succeed. To be competent a person would need to be able to interpret the situation in the context and to have a repertoire of possible actions to take and have trained in the possible actions in the repertoire, if this is relevant. Regardless of training, competency would grow through experience and the extent of an individual to learn and adapt.

Competency has different meanings, and continues to remain one of the most diffuse terms in the management development sector, and the organizational and occupational literature.[1]

Competencies are also what people need to be successful in their jobs. Job competencies are not the same as job tasks. Competencies include all the related knowledge, skills, abilities, and attributes that form a person's job. This set of context-specific qualities is correlated with superior job performance and can be used as a standard against which to measure job performance as well as to develop, recruit, and hire employees.*

*Wikipedia® is a registered trademark of the Wikimedia Foundation, Inc., a non-profit organization. (Cited from source-Wikipedia- July 8, 2015)

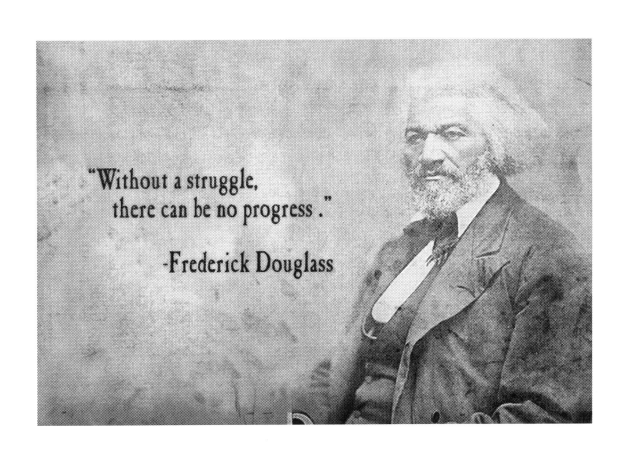

UNIT 1:

Employee Literacy

A WISE WORD….

"After all is said and done; after we talk, and commensurate about what our lives really mean and what is essential to everyday living we will always come to the undeniable reality that we deal with and exist in life in a financial way. We buy and consume. Whatever our vocation or contribution to the world we have to eat, we have to have a roof over our head, and for most of us we have to pay bills. No money, no honey. It is that simple. Having financial knowledge is necessary for day-day survival. We cannot chance life without financial knowledge. To know about our money is to know more about the life we live because our access to life as we know it is tied to finance in some way, shape, form or fashion." (Reed, 2014)

Discussion

1. What point do you think Mr. Reed is trying to make?
2. Why do you think what he said is important?
3. Does this apply to you?

_____

_____

_____

_____

_____

_____

_____

_____

_____

So let's begin!!!!

1. EMPLOYEE LITERACY:

(A definition) Knowledge, understanding and practice of job related skills and expertise. This knowledge is developed to acquire, maintain and excel in an employment opportunity.

We will begin with a question. How do you rate yourself, using this definition?

Let's start with the goal in mind. The goal is to learn how to be a valued employee. We will measure the attainment of the goal by our definition of "employee literacy".

2. WHAT DOES EMPLOYMENT MEAN?

Word IQ.com defines it this way: **Employment** is a <u>contract</u> between two parties, one being the **employer** and the other being the **employee**. In a commercial setting, the employer conceives of a productive activity, generally with the intention of creating <u>profits</u>, and the employee contributes <u>labour</u> to the <u>enterprise</u>, usually in return for payment of <u>wages</u>.

Why this definition?

We believe that while this definition tells part of the story, in and of itself it does not truly paint the whole picture. We submit employment represents security, for families and for our nation as a whole. We believe that it represents the value of being productive and gainful…a contributing, fully participating member of society. We believe that for most of us, our employment or lack thereof defines us in a way like no other activity in our life. (RIM GROUP)

Question: Did you ever wonder why the first question that people ask you when they meet you is; "so what do you do for a living?"

So now that we have a working definition of employment, let's dig deeper.

3. ASSESSING ABILITIES: EDUCATION, SKILLS, APTITUDES (KNOWING YOURSELF…MAKING YOURSELF THE BEST YOU CAN BE)

Our society places value on many things. Knowledge is valuable in all societies. That knowledge as relates to employment begins with self. We must know our strengths, weaknesses and what skills we possess in order to be gainfully employed. In his October 2013 article "Money Talk" Leslie D. Reed said it this way:

"I leave you with a simple formula. We all need money, so if that is the case we have some choices. Get trained & more educated to make ourselves more valuable in the employment marketplace. 2. If we can't get more training or education, than quite simply we have to get more employment (a 2nd job). 3. We can become the employer ourselves and create a business or enterprise from our available skills and talents...than we become the employer". (Scoop Magazine, Indianapolis October 9, 2013)

So we must ask and face the hard question of: What kinds of job do I quality for? Do I have the necessary skill sets/aptitudes?

Discussion:

1. Does everyone have to get a college degree?

_____

_____

_____

_____

2. What is the background and training of a typical millionaire?

_____

_____

_____

_____

3. Can a person overcome having formal training in today's workplace? (examples)

_____

_____

_____

_____

4. GETTING A JOB (THIS IS WHERE THE WORK BEGINS)

Getting a job usually starts at the application stage. Nowadays that application is online (usually). For the purposes of this seminar we will look at applications generally, with no distinction between online or in person applications. Note: If your computer skills are limited, you may want to take a basic class. They are offered free at most libraries. Minimally, have a friend help you out…**NO EXCUSES!!!**

A good application will:

- Be typed or written legibly (if your words aren't understood…)
- Be accurate, tell the truth, concisely. Don't over answer!
- Keep a record of your job experiences (all applications ask this)
- Know all prior addresses
- Make sure you qualify for the job that you are applying for
- Have up to date references that can be contacted (current phone number & address)
- Not have scratch outs (someone else is reading this…don't eliminate yourself this way).

Special Consideration: If there are legal circumstances that you have to reveal you should:

*Be clear about the dates, times and circumstances surrounding your issues. Check out what laws are current in your locality. Your record (if old) may be eligible for expungement. In all cases where you have to answer, be honest. Employers consider this. You may get a chance to explain in an interview.

Discussion:

1. Do you think that these points are too stringent?

_____

_____

_____

_____

2. Do you feel the questions are too intrusive?

_____

_____

_____

_____

3. Why do you think an employer needs to know all this?

_____

_____

_____

_____

Now that we have applied for the job, let's move on to the interview.

The interview is the most critical phase of your job search. Having the right skills will make or break your chances for employment.

Interview Etiquette:

Let's agree on one basic rule. If what you say, what you do, or what you look like can offend, then don't say it, do it, or wear it!!! NO EXCUSES!!!

Before the interview:

- ❖ Know something about the company and position you are applying for
- ❖ Be rested and arrive on time
- ❖ Go in with the mindset that you are the best candidate for the job!

-Wear an appropriate outfit, Ladies tasteful, and moderately conservative. Gentleman, suit or at least shirt & tie (if you can, avoid excessive or conspicuous styles) be appropriately groomed. If you don't have the right clothes, borrow them. **NO EXCUSES!**

In the Interview:

- ❖ Sit upright but not uncomfortably
- ❖ Speak clearly, answer the question you are being asked…don't over embellish
- ❖ Use the King's English
- ❖ Ask appropriate questions about the position/company
- ❖ If you don't understand a question, politely ask the interviewer to repeat it
- ❖ As the interview concludes, ask about next steps. If there is only one interview, ASK FOR THE JOB!!

Resume Tip

"The Skills Selection gives you total control over how you're perceived by employers. Without this section, you're basically a victim of your work experience and education."

Discussion:

1. If I have a great application and job experience, why is the interview just as important?

_____

_____

_____

_____

2. Why should I ask questions in an interview?

_____

_____

_____

_____

3. Why should I ask for the job?

_____

_____

_____

_____

Now we have the job, what's next?

5. KEEPING A JOB & YOUR WORK ETHIC (WORKPLACE PRIMER)

COMMENTARY:

We have all been there. You are at the restaurant or business and the person greets you (most times sounding practiced and routine) and then they turn and start talking to one of their associates. You are standing there and they are carrying on a conversation as if you aren't there. How about this: you are in the line and there are several people behind the counter and no one waits on you. Sound familiar? It happens every day, and we as a society have become immune to it. Maybe I've got it wrong but there seems to be an attitude that we are "entitled" to our job. Or better, "it's just a minimum wage job so why should I care?" Is this you? This next section will deal with the dynamic of keeping a job, "your work ethic".

Top Interview Questions

1. What is your greatest strength?
2. What is your greatest weakness?
3. Why are you leaving or have left your job?
4. Tell me about yourself.
5. Why do you want this job?
6. Why should we hire you?
7. How do you handle stress and pressure?
8. Describe a difficult work situation / project and how you overcame it.
9. How do you evaluate success?
10. What are your goals for the future?

Sample Answers

1. I have an extremely strong work ethic. When I'm working on a project, I don't want just to meet deadlines. Rather, I prefer to complete the project well ahead of schedule. Last year, I even earned a bonus for completing my three most recent reports one week ahead of time.

2. When I'm working on a project, I don't want just to meet deadlines. Rather, I prefer to complete the project well ahead of schedule.

3. I found myself bored with the work and looking for more challenges. I am an excellent employee and I didn't want my unhappiness to have any impact on the job I was doing for my employer.

4. Avoid politics and controversy, transition from personal to professional, and share your expertise.

5. I understand that this is a company on the way up. Your web site says the launch of several new products is imminent. I want be a part of this business as it grows.

6. You describe in the job listing that you are looking for a special education assistant teacher with an abundance of patience and compassion. Having served as a tutor at a summer school for dyslexic children for the past two years, I have developed my ability to be extremely patient while still achieving academic gains with my students. My experience teaching phonics to children ages 6 to 18 has taught me strategies for working with children of all ages and abilities, always with a smile. My previous employer often placed me with the students with the most severe learning disabilities

because of my history of success. I will bring not only experience, but patience and creative problem-solving, to this position.

7. I react to situations, rather than to stress. That way, the situation is handled and doesn't become stressful.

8. Keep your answers positive ("Even though it was difficult when Jane Doe quit without notice, we were able to rearrange the department workload to cover the position until a replacement was hired.") and be specific. Itemize what you did and how you did it.

9. For me, success is about doing my job well. I want to be recognized as someone who always does their best and tries their hardest to make my goals."

10. My long-term goals involve growing with a company where I can continue to learn, take on additional responsibilities, and contribute as much of value as I can.

Keeping your job is vital. For you, for your family. But how about making your job more than a job? How about doing so well at your job that you improve your opportunity for promotion. For making your skill portable (move to other jobs). All of this translates into more money for you and your family. Isn't this the objective?

At your job you should:

- Arrive early…arriving on time is late. You are not ready to work!
- Avoid excessive conversation, you are here to work.
- Make sure you understand the duties of your job.
- Be presentable!
- Don't think of where you are in your job, think of where your job will take you.
- Deal with customers/public as if you value them. (they are the reason you have a job)
- Don't get caught up in the politics of the workplace (politics are everywhere, you are here to perform a job).
- Focus on the job at hand.
- Perform your job to the best of your ability (give 100%)
- Reduce your personality. (Be a team player)
- Do things without being asked.

This all may seem simple but we all know that it doesn't take place. BE DIFFERENT! MAKE YOUR JOB WORK FOR YOU! It will translate into a bigger paycheck!

Discussion:

1. Why should I be at work early, they only pay me for the time I am scheduled?

_____

_____

_____

_____

_____

2. It is a minimum wage job, why should I work hard?

_____

_____

_____

_____

3. How can I make my job work for me?

_____

_____

_____

_____

So far we have learned about getting and keeping a job. This leads us to the end game of having a job and becoming a valued employee! Keep in mind, our personal financial goal is the well being of our family and those we love (see previous comments) Along with this goal is the equally important goal for the company- Continued growth that leads to a continued paycheck for you!

6. BECOMING A VALUED EMPLOYEE….GROWING AS AN EMPLOYEE

Commentary:

Too often we see things as what's in it for me. This is fine and good, but we must learn that it's not "all about me". We believe that if a person learns to make his whole situation better, he makes his personal situation better. Translation; the more valuable you are to your employer, the more valuable you are to yourself. Many of the jobs we get are just "stops on the road". We have to quit thinking of what someone is getting from us and start believing that our value to our employer and workplace is a transferable value. Quality, hard work, and dependability will always be rewarded. It will always have a place in the working world. Believe it or not, becoming a valued employee will in the end be in your best interest As the book evolves we will discuss the employee as a part of the "profit outlook". In this discussion we will talk about the employees goals and how they should line up with the goals of the company. Ultimately increased productivity and profits should be everyone's goal. **NO EXCUSES!**

Becoming a valued employee means:

❖ Understanding your job and performing it at the highest level.
❖ Doing what others aren't willing to do.
❖ Be there before your boss gets there; stay there after your boss leaves
❖ Be willing to learn and take on more responsibilities
❖ Understand the duties of the job at the next level (your boss)
❖ Think of yourself as a business: "how do I improve my brand"

- ❖ Understand how your company makes money; buy into it! Own it! Contribute to the "profit picture"
- ❖ Help your company cut expenses and save money
- ❖ Be irreplaceable!

Discussion:

1. Why should I be concerned with my boss making more money?

_____

_____

_____

_____

2. Why is "my brand" so important?

_____

_____

_____

_____

3. Why should I do more than my job calls for?

_____

_____

_____

_____

7 TRANSLATING EMPLOYEE LITERACY INTO GREATER PRODUCTIVITY & PROFIT

Commentary:

So far we have learned about getting and keeping a job. This leads to having a job. Then, becoming a valued employee! Keep in mind; our personal goal is the well being of our family and those we love (see previous comments) Along with this goal is the equally important goal for the company: Continued growth that leads to a continued paycheck for you! Your paycheck depends on the company producing a great product/service, and PROFITABILITY!!! This should be your end game. In this section we will translate what we've learned to see how everyone benefits. (Win/Win)

Translating employee literacy means:

- Seeing yourself as responsible for the companies goals/objectives
- Understanding that your productivity is how the company survives
- How well you treat customers translates to increased company profitability
- Great morale & comradery in the workplace is paramount to business success
- Understanding your specific role in the scheme of the company's mission
- Seeing yourself as an "entrepreneur" within the company
- Viewing your job as an opportunity: it may or may not work out with your current company. This is fine, but are your skills portable? Would you bring value anywhere you worked?
- Do you share the company's mission and values?
- Is this a better company because you are here?
- Consistently demonstrating the habits and work ethic that make you/company competitive in the marketplace
- Do I understand that increased profits =promotions=raises=matching 401(k) contributions by my employer?

Let's sum it up this way:

"WHO MAKES THE MOST MONEY AN EMPLOYEE OR AN EMPLOYER? WHO TAKES THE RISK OF OWNERSHIP THE EMPLOYEE OR THE OWNER? IN THE END THIS EQUATION APPLIES TO THE EMPLOYEE AND THE EMPLOYER…. IF YOU LOOK AT THIS EQUATION ANY OTHER WAY YOU ARE CHEATING YOUR COMPANY, BUT MORE IMPORTANTLY…YOURSELF!!! THIS IS THE END GAME OF "EMPLOYEE" LITERACY…IT IS WIN/WIN… (RIM GROUP, 2013)

Discussion:

1. What can I do to think/act more like an entrepreneur in my company?

_____

_____

_____

_____

2. On the job how do I take into account more than just a paycheck?

_____

_____

_____

_____

3. Do I communicate to my employer what my goals and aspirations are (where do I want to go in this company…in life?)

_____

_____

_____

_____

8. PAYOFF:

There is absolutely nothing wrong with wanting more money. We submit that it is the "American Way". This section of the book deals with employment because for most of us it is the resource that we all have. It is inescapable. This being the case, we should work to make ourselves the best employee we can be. Employment means many things, but in the end it is how we take care of our family. It is how we build a home and a future. Even more than just the financial aspect of a job, doing well on our job creates for us greater self worth, improved lifestyle, and ultimately contributes to us being a well adjusted, thriving human being. If we look at our jobs as just "a job", that is all we will get out of it. If we become great at getting a job, keeping a job, and becoming a "valued employee," we will be rewarded. It is true spiritually and practically. You are a product/service in and of yourself. See yourself that way. Get all that you deserve. Make what you do for a living as excellent as you want others to see you. It will prove to be valuable not only to you, but to anyone who may need you as employee in the future. It's your brand, grow it and develop it. Make yourself valuable. Get all that you deserve.

UNIT 2:

"DYNAMICS OF MONEY & MONEY MANAGEMENT"

A WISE WORD…..

"A penny saved is a penny earned". This quote is often attributed to Benjamin Franklin; it seems it is only quoted partially right. Here is the original quote: "A penny saved is two pence dear".

Most of us know that Benjamin Franklin lived a long time ago, but the truth is, what he said then is still true today.

Discussion:

1. What do you think the revised quote means?

_____

_____

_____

_____

2. Is it how much money you make or how much money you keep?

_____

_____

_____

_____

3. Do most people live beyond their means?

_____

_____

_____

_____

Unit 2:

DYNAMICS OF MONEY & MONEY MANAGEMENT:

(A definition) Knowledge, understanding and practice of money related skills. These skills include, budgeting, spending habits, growth of money=loaning/owning of money, insurance protection, retirement planning and wealth transfer. This knowledge developed to obtain, maintain, grow and transfer your financial assets. (RIM GROUP, 2013)

We will begin again with a question. How do you rate yourself using this definition?

Let's start with the goal in mind. The goal is to manage your finances in a manner that you can afford and enjoy the lifestyle you desire. We will measure the attainment of the goal by our definition of "dynamics of money & money management".

WHAT DOES MONEY MANAGEMENT MEAN?

"The process of budgeting, saving, spending, or otherwise overseeing cash usage of an individual or group". Investopedia

BUDGETING

There are two basic components of a budget: Income or revenue and expenses or costs.

1. The income component is combining all of the money you make from all income sources to come up with the amount of money you have to pay your expenses and costs.
2. The expense component is combining all you owe and deciding whether it is a current expense or something that must be paid in the future.

Knowledge of what you spend is critical to having a budget that is realistic and effective. Living within your budget is the way you make the budget work.

-1ˢᵗ step is writing down or keeping receipts for every dollar you spend…every dollar! To have the best budget you should do this for three months. This will give you a long enough time to see what and how you spend.

- 2ⁿᵈ step is sorting your expenses into expenses you pay every month (fixed) and which expenses you pay bi-monthly, quarterly or otherwise.

-3ʳᵈ step is looking at all of the remaining expenses that you have kept track of over the last 3 months and eliminating the ones that are not necessary.(discuss briefly)

-4ᵗʰ step is budgeting for some incidental expenses such as entertainment, travel (gas) and emergencies. (Discuss Briefly)

-5ᵗʰ step is estimate variable expenses (as much as you can)

This exercise should give you a good idea of "how you spend money". With this knowledge you will then have to make some decisions.

- Do I make enough to cover my expenses?
- Do I have enough to budget for incidentals?
- Do I have room in my budget for savings?

Once these questions are decided, you can put your budget in place. There will be a final step.

Revising, updating and reviewing your budget and how well you are staying with it!

Many things can change in your in your economic picture, your job, unexpected bills, or income. In order to address them you have to manage your budget. This is an ongoing process.

The success of your budget does not lie in making a budget; your budget's success lies in allowing it to be the guide that sets up the foundation of all of your finances. With this in place you can now start on the next phase, which is saving.

Discussion:

1. Why does forming a budget take time?

_____

_____

_____

_____

2. Why budget for incidentals and entertainment?

_____

_____

_____

_____

BANKING RELATIONSHIP (ESTABLISHING & MAINTAINING A CHECKING ACCOUNT)

Establishing and maintaining a checking account is the foundation of your financial house. It will allow you to pay your bills without carrying cash; by using a check or debit card. In today's financial world where so many transactions are online, by phone, or do not use a check, it is critical that you have a banking relationship with a reputable bank. Your checking account can function as your "bookkeeper" if used correctly. It can document all of your income and expenses in one place. It can also be useful as you prepare your taxes. The function and need for a checking account cannot be overstated.

CHECKING ACCOUNT DEFINED (DEMAND DEPOSIT ACCOUNT)

"An account which allows the holder to write checks against deposited funds".

Discussion:

What are components of a written check: **(DDAMPE)**

- Drawer

_____

_____

_____

- Date

_____

_____

_____

- Amount

_____

_____

_____

- Payee

_____

_____

_____

- Endorsement

_____

_____

_____

Now that we know how to write a check, as well as a check's components, let's discuss the critical exercise of checkbook balancing.

BALANCING YOUR CHECKBOOK (RECONCILIATION)

Balancing your checkbook is essential and it is relatively easy if you follow the basic steps. After you start your checking account and make the first deposit, your banking institution should review with you the basics of having a checking account. At this point you should pay attention to checks you write, deposits you make, fees you may incur, and when you receive your monthly account statement.

Your meeting with your banker and what comes after the 1ˢᵗ deposit:

-discuss with the banker the different checking account options. Many times you can open a free checking account with direct deposit of a payroll or other check. Discuss with the banker the amount of checks you think you will write, as well as deposits you might make. This is important as it is what will determine the amount of fees you will be charged.

KEY POINT: THE BANK WANTS YOUR DEPOSITS BECAUSE THIS IS THE BUSINESS THEY ARE IN. YOUR MONEY IS YOUR BUSINESS, SO IT IS IMPORTANT THAT YOU PAY ATTENTION TO THE FEES AND CHARGES ASSOCIATED WITH A BANK ACCOUNT. THE MONEY YOU SAVE IN FEES AND CHARGES STAYS IN YOUR POCKET. UNDERSTAND YOU ARE THE BUSINESS!!

- Ask the banker what the cost of printed checks are (you can get checks from other sources but doing it when you open your account is easiest)
- Enter the amount of the 1ˢᵗ deposit in your check register
- Deduct the amount of the check printing expense from your 1ˢᵗ deposit
- **THIS IS YOUR BEGINNING BALANCE.**

- When you write a check, record the amount in your register, subtracting the check amount from your balance. This will give you a new balance.
- Use online banking or telephone banking periodically to see which checks have cleared your bank (been paid), which is also called getting the activity on your account, and match this against your own checkbook. If you are keeping an accurate check register they should be the same. (It is always good to know what the "bank says" is going on with your account). They make mistakes to, but it is your responsibility to know about "your account" and your money!!!
- When you get your statement, "reconcile with the bank". This means:

1. Check the balance in your check register with the balance your bank statement shows. If you have followed the previous steps they should be the same, with any difference being the service charge (if any).
2. Match the checks that the bank shows as clearing your account against your check register. If they are the same you are finished, if they are not DO NOT write checks against the bank statement balance, use your balance instead.

3. If you notice discrepancies between what your register shows and what is on the bank statement, check out your account online or by phone. If there is a discrepancy, visit your bank as soon possible to clear it up.

4. If you have followed these steps, your bank account should be accurate and up to date.

These steps are simple and require a little effort on your part, but establishing and maintaining a good banking relationship is good money management, and will also help your overall credit score (discussed later).

Discussion:

1. Do you think having a banking account is necessary?

_____

_____

_____

_____

2. What do you think is the most common error people make with their checking account?

_____

_____

_____

_____

3. Why is a checking account referred to as a "Demand Deposit Account"?

_____

_____

_____

4. Should I have overdraft protection on my account?

_____

_____

_____

_____

CREDIT MANAGEMENT:

Wise word:

"Those who have money typically use it to advantage against those that don't. Those who borrow are typically at the mercy of those who lend."

COMMENTARY:

Credit: It is, important and necessary. If you own a car, a home, or a business, you probably have used credit. Credit is not just for everyday people: credit is used by practically everybody from individuals with low and average income, to the wealthiest of people. Credit is not just about money; it is also "social" matter. Whether we like it or not or whether it is fair or not, the use and or misuse of credit is pervasive: it touches our life in many ways. Most people are aware of credit reports, and credit bureaus. They are also aware of credit scores. We will deal with the use of credit from a positive stand point: the use of credit to enhance your life, and how it can be used properly to maximize your financial power and enhance your life. We will discuss credit from the standpoint of a lender and what the lender looks for when he extends credit. Let's say it this way: credit was created for good reasons, it is up to us to understand how those reasons can be good for us.

CREDIT DEFINED:

1. A contractual agreement in which a borrower receives something of value now and agrees to repay the lender at some later date.

2. Let's say it another way: Belief or confidence in the truth of something. Credit is the same as your word!!!

LENDER OR CREDITORS VIEW:

Why is credit extended?

- ➤ lender charges interest, which is income for their lending business
- ➤ gives businesses the necessary capitol to help their business grow
- ➤ allows individuals to make purchases such as homes and cars that would otherwise be unobtainable

➢ is essential to the creating the "flow of money" that our economy needs"

➢ when businesses and individuals thrive: banks and lenders get more deposits

Discussion:

1. What is the flow of money?

_____

_____

_____

_____

2. How does lending money end up increasing a banks or lending institutions deposits?

_____

_____

_____

_____

3. Should I have credit?

_____

_____

_____

_____

CREDIT: BASIC TERMINOLOGY

5 C's of Credit= the five key elements a borrower should have to obtain credit:

❖ Character (integrity)
❖ Capacity (sufficient cash flow to service the obligation)
❖ Capital (net worth)
❖ Collateral (assets to secure the debt)
❖ Conditions (of the borrower and the overall economy)

We gave two different definitions of credit previously because the true meaning of credit encompasses both. It is a financial matter; it is a confidence or trust matter. The 5 C's of credit deal with the subjective aspect of credit. This cannot be overlooked.

FINANCIAL LEVERAGE: (WHY WE NEED & USE CREDIT)

The degree to which an investor or business is utilizing borrowed money. Companies or individuals that are highly leveraged may be at risk of bankruptcy if they are unable to make payments on their debt; they may be also be unable to find new lenders in the future. Financial leverage is not always bad, however, it can increase an individual or businesses return on investment and often there are tax advantages associated with borrowing….also called **LEVERAGE.**

What does this definition really mean? (From an individual's standpoint)

There is a reason for people to use credit: For emergencies, large purchases that can be paid over time, for temporary cash flow issues. The key to credit is the same as all other aspects of your financial situation. It is MANAGEMENT!! Credit should be utilized within the context of your whole financial situation. We should not borrow more than we can reasonably pay back…in a reasonable time. The payback should not be so much that it disrupts our <u>cash flow</u> **(a measure of your financial health: it equals cash you bring, minus cash you pay out over a given time).**

In Summary: Credit is useful and necessary at times. It has its place and can be a wonderful financial tool if utilized properly. If used incorrectly, it can damage your credit rating, and have other long term negative effects that diminish financial health and ultimately, your well being.

Discussion:

- 5 C's of Credit
- Financial Leverage
- Good/Bad uses of credit
- What is a credit reporting agency?
- Who are they? How do I get a copy of my credit report?
- How do I read my credit report?
- What does credit score mean?

SAVING:

The savings portion of your finances and budget is crucial because it sets the foundation of stability and growth in your finances. The importance of savings should be understood as a bridge to improving your financial situation. It will help in 3 key ways:

1. Savings will allow you to maintain the budget you have in place to:
   - ❖ Have funds for emergencies
   - ❖ Give you the needed resources should your employment situation change
   - ❖ Allow you to make spending decisions with less stress

2. Having savings will give you more control of the choices you make as you improve your financial situation:
   - ❖ You will develop the skill of controlling unnecessary spending
   - ❖ You will have the flexibility of making "unplanned" purchases that might be necessary

3. Having savings is the first step towards understanding how to start making your money make money for you.
   - ❖ You will have more options in making investments
   - ❖ You will be able to allow your investments the time it takes for them to payoff
   - ❖ You will grow your overall understanding of how money can work for you.

Think of it as a cycle: You make money....Then you manage your money.... Then you learn how to make your money make more money for you.

Final thought: We can sum up this section with an affirmation to keep us on track: **IT'S NOT WHAT YOU MAKE...IT'S WHAT YOU KEEP!**

We have a need and duty to not just have money but be good stewards of the money we have. This is not just to maintain our money at its current level; it is having our money grow as well. Having money is only partially doing the job!

Here we will look at the options most of us have to make more money with our money. We need to get a basic understanding of how money grows. There are two fundamental money making concepts:

1. **Loaning money:** said another way: it is earning interest on your money via a savings/ money market account type of account. You in effect allow a bank/institution to take your money on deposit and give you interest for the time your money stays with them.

The advantages of this method are:

- Your money is generally safer
- You will earn a guaranteed rate of return
- Easier to understand and manage

The disadvantages are:

- Savings rates are low currently. You will not make a lot of money
- When the rate of inflation is higher than what you earn on your money you are effectively "losing money"
- Will require you to save more money to reach your financial goals

2. **Owning Money:** said another way; growing your money by investment, be it stocks, bonds, real estate or any investment that you make, takes more time to grow.

The advantages of this method are;

- The value of your investment can grow more than a standard savings/money market account.
- You have more options in how you grow your money
- You will expand your knowledge of different financial instruments, thus improving your chances to earn more with your money
- In most cases your money will grow more than inflation

The disadvantages of this method are:

- The value of your investments can fluctuate
- You will have to invest more time in improving your knowledge of these types of investments.
- Making more money will cause you to pay more taxes and be more tax savvy.

How does owning and loaning money work together?

We will use this phrase to summarize the relationship of loaning and owning money. **RISK/REWARD.**

This is the most critical equation you must understand!!

*When we loan money (put it in savings types of accounts) we are putting funds in a place with little to no risk, but we are willing to accept less return for the taking less risk.

*When we own money (put it in investments that fluctuate at times) we are putting our money in a place with more risk, but we are giving our money a chance for greater returns.

The key than is to understand how you perceive and accept risk. Going back to the essence of the equation, you have to understand that just maintaining your money is not enough. This doesn't mean just putting your money in investments that grow the most. It is understanding that you have to consider and learn that there is a balance between both ways of growing your money, and then figuring out where you stand as far as how you will manage that risk/ reward equation.

The equation is encouraging us to truly consider the value of growing our money as being a good steward of it. The more you learn about how the money you make can be properly used to increase your financial well being, the more you are being the right steward of your money.

Discussion:

1. How do we access resources to learn more about "growing our money?"

_____

_____

_____

_____

2. What do I do if I can't deal with fluctuations in my money?

_____

_____

_____

_____

3. When is it too later to start this part of the process?

_____

_____

_____

_____

4. What is the difference in a savings account versus stocks/bonds or real estate?

_____

_____

_____

_____

A WISE WORD….Most people dream of the day when they can have "money in the bank". It creates a different comfort level in your life. Getting to a few thousand dollars in the bank will take some effort, but when you see it…..you find that you are "ahead" of most problems. You can maintain without that anxious feeling of not knowing how to handle life's unexpected financial difficulties. To see a million dollars you have to first see hundreds then thousands. Once you "see it" the light of a new way of living will shine in your life….why not you? (Ron Robinson, 2013 paraphrased)

LIFE INSURANCE PROTECTION & RETIREMENT SAVINGS

Dealing with your money and finances is an ongoing process that requires many phases to make for a complete and thorough plan. Having a basic understanding of life insurance protection and retirement savings is necessary. These two elements, like the others will require resources and time to implement. In order to be "financially literate" you must at least understand basically how these two elements affect your planning and your results. For our purposes here we will talk about these from a basic framework, while giving you a way to include these in your plans using resources that you may have access to right now.

The basic types of life insurance are:

1. Whole Life or permanent insurance:

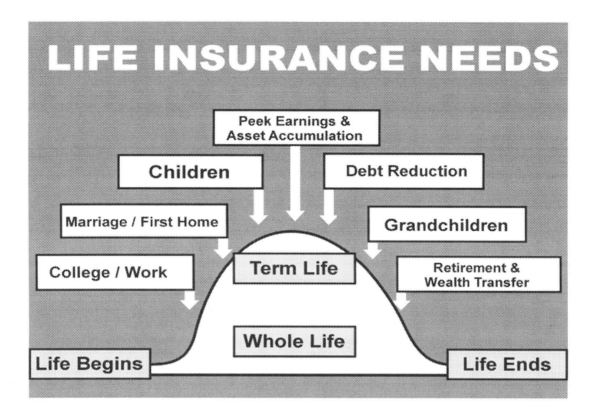

Advantages are:

- Once established your cost or premium will stay the same, regardless of any changes in your health
- Can build cash value
- Can serve as an additional source of cash (can be borrowed against)

Disadvantages are:

- More costly than term insurance
- Does not earn a high rate of return

2. Term Life Insurance:

Advantages are:

- Less expensive than whole life
- Provides the same coverage as whole life
- Can be converted to permanent insurance

Disadvantages are:

- Builds no cash value
- Covers only a set period of time. Usually 10, 20, or 30 year period.
- When the term runs out, you will have to prove insurability again

RETIREMENT SAVINGS:

Most people are able to start a retirement savings plan with an employer who offers a retirement plan. For our purposes we will talk about the most popular plan: 401 (k) and briefly discuss IRA's for those who don't have the ability to use a 401(k) plan.

401(k) Plans

Advantages are:
- Uses pretax dollars (you don't pay taxes on money you put in the plan)
- Generally there is a matching contribution made by your employer
- Most plans offer investments that you might not have access to outside of a 401(k)
- Payroll deduction feature makes investing automatic

Disadvantages are:
- For many plans, there is no one to advise you concerning investment choices
- Most plan choices involve some risk
- You will not have access to your money without incurring penalties to withdraw
- Will require more time to manage

IRA's (Regular Individual Retirement Account)

This type of retirement account is available to you whether or not your company has a retirement plan or not. As the name suggest, it is a retirement account in your individual name and it is used as a retirement savings account.

Advantages are:
- In most cases uses pre-tax dollars
- Many plans have a variety of investment options
- Some employers can give you the ability to make your contributions through payroll deductions.

- IRA's are offered at banks and through investment companies where you can get advice on what to invest in.
- The rules on transferring your accounts and withdrawals are more flexible

Disadvantages are:
- No employer match
- Early withdrawals will incur taxes and penalties (before age 59 ½)
- Lower contribution limits

Final points on Life Insurance & Retirement Savings

We mentioned previously that there is a way that most of us can gain access to life insurance protection and retirement savings: Through our employer. This is not always the case but when you do have access (you should inquire) it can give your financial plan a serious advantage. **Part of your financial literacy is learning what benefits are available to you. And getting the maximum benefit from resources you already hav**e. Most employer plans are attractive because:

- they are generally less expensive than doing it on your own
- in the case of retirement savings, many employers will match what you put in
- most employers understand the long term benefits of offering their employees these types of benefits (we will discuss this more in later sections)

Discussion:

1. Why do I have to be aware of investments besides a savings account?

_____

_____

_____

_____

2. Why is insurance considered a part of financial literacy?

_____

_____

_____

_____

3. Why should I worry about retirement savings?

_____

_____

_____

_____

WEALTH TRANSFER

Defined: Wealth transfer is a term used to describe the transfer of money from one individual to others, typically after or in anticipation of the death of the person whose wealth is being distributed. Many people with significant funds start planning for wealth transfer long before death, because distributing wealth is often subject to complex taxes that can be avoided by starting early. People without many financial assets should still look into some form of planning to distribute wealth upon death...... source: wise geek

Commentary:

We have all heard the phrase "born with a silver spoon in their mouth"; well there is more truth to this phrase then fable. Our work so far has taken us from earning money, creating a budget, to how we make our money grow for day-day living up to retirement. We touched on Life insurance for protection, now we will use this information to understand the last phase in money dynamics, wealth transfer. Back to the phrase we started with. Financial literacy doesn't end with making money or your retirement. There is a reason some people are born with a silver spoon in their mouth; it's called wealth transfer. The truth about wealth transfer is simple. We shouldn't work all our lives to die and all of our efforts do nothing for our children, grandchildren or even our community. The cycle of poverty and lack can be changed generationally. It is done by planning. By planning, families are able to create a foundation of economic stability that can make it easier for those they leave behind. Our thinking has to change from what's in it for me to how can the financial efforts of my life transcend my living. Offspring don't ask to be here, and true wealth is created over generations. Your actions are part of that continuum. This phase of learning about our finances is necessary….and reasonable. Wealth transfer is not just the province of the rich….we all need it and should have access to it. Life insurance, which we all can access, can aid us in this process. The legacy of our country is that the next generation should do better than the previous one. This phase allows us to do just that. With this in mind let's take a look at the dynamics of this process. We will not deal with all of the complexities of estate planning wills etc…, just how life insurance can play a role in this process.

BENEFITS OF WEALTH TRANSFER PLANNING WITH LIFE INSURANCE

Most people do not have assets so large that they need highly technical wealth transfer planning. For the cost of a life insurance premium you can effectively pass your assets to your heirs or the beneficiary you choose with the following benefits:

Less expensive…your cost is the life insurance policy. Note: the cost of life insurance is aged based. The earlier in life you get it, the less expensive.

Simplicity…..once you have the life insurance policy, you just choose your beneficiary, that's it!

The death benefit from a life insurance policy passes to your heirs/family INCOME TAX FREE.

Peace of mind knowing today, what your family will receive in the future.

Possible tax advantages if you have sizeable assets.

Create instant wealth for your family

Discussion:

1. Why should I create wealth for my children to have when I'm gone?

_____

_____

_____

_____

2. How do I decide who my beneficiaries should be?

_____

_____

_____

_____

3. Should I discuss this with my family?

_____

_____

_____

_____

4. Can I help my church or charity by using life insurance?

_____

_____

_____

_____

TAX REFUNDS (RETURN) USING IT EFFECTIVELY

COMMENTARY:

Getting a tax refund check is one of the greatest financial highlights for most people. In fact, for most of us it is the largest check or lump sum of money that we receive in our lifetime. If used responsibly, it can be a powerful tool in your financial arsenal. The following are some thoughts and guidelines on tax refunds that can save you some money and help you make proper use of this asset that you receive (in most cases) every year. To say it another way, "use your money (tax refund) don't let it use you". We will not attempt to explore all of the nuances of tax preparation or tax law: our goal is to give you some pointers on tax preparation and better use of your tax refund.

Tax Refund defined: "The return of excess amounts of income tax that a taxpayer has paid to the state or federal government throughout the past year. In certain cases, taxpayers may even receive a refund if they owed no taxes, because certain tax credits are fully refundable" (investopedia 2013).

Tax Preparation:

Getting your taxes prepared professionally is a good idea, and in most cases should afford you a greater return than if you prepare them yourself. If you prepare them yourself, the tax booklet provided by the IRS will give you a line by line explanation of what to do and where to go in the tax booklet to answer any question you may have. This obviously involves some time and some knowledge on your part. You can also purchase tax preparation software, which in most cases is relatively easy to navigate. In any of these cases, you should attempt to learn what you can about your tax situation, and ask questions about how you can get the biggest return and/or pay the least tax.

Points To Consider:

- The fee you pay to have your taxes prepared should not be excessively high. Put another way, if it takes the preparer more time, resources and they file more forms it will cost you more. Conversely, if you have a simple return you should not pay a high fee. Always negotiate the fee you pay. This is absolutely ok.
- Tax Anticipation Loans are EXPENSIVE. You should know that if you can be a little patient about when you get your return, it could save you hundreds of dollars. If your return is e-filed by you or a preparer, you can usually expect your refund in 7-10 days. This is average, but the point is, waiting a little longer keeps more money in your pocket.
- Be Organized!! The more organized you are the easier it is to prepare your return, which translates into a quicker return.

WHEN YOU RECEIVE YOUR TAX REFUND:

The most important thing to remember about your return is to mange it wisely. Here are some tips to consider.

- It's ok to pay off some debts, but don't use all of your return for this. Target high interest debt first.
- This is a way to establish your "rainy day" fund (emergency fund). What you will end up finding out is, if you have funds for a rainy day, it usually doesn't come.
- This is a good time to establish an IRA
- Plan to "keep" more of your refund by budgeting and watching how you spend money all year. Don't spend and use money frivolously just because you know you have a tax refund coming.

Discussion:

1. When should I review my tax withholding with my employer?

_____

_____

_____

_____

2. Does the state or local government pay me interest before I get my tax refund?

_____

_____

_____

_____

3. What is the difference in tax credits and items that reduce my taxable income?

_____

_____

_____

_____

4. Why is earned income so important?

_____

_____

_____

_____

UNIT 3:

EMPLOYER LITERACY

Defined: **"The knowledge and understanding that an employment situation is not a one sided relationship of an employer employing another; it is a two sided relationship that benefits both parties. It includes profits and company growth for the employer; it also includes the employee embracing the same values as an employer such that he sees his value tied to more than just maintaining a job. The employee embraces a mentality that acknowledges increased productivity, company growth of profits and his well being as being aligned with the employer. Once the employee operates in this attitude, his value to the employment situation increases and he gains skills and knowledge that are transferable to any employment situation. This relationship creates the win/win that any employer or employee is seeking and should be the ultimate goal of both. Ultimately both parties gain and businesses grow, thrive and profit"... (RIM Group, 2013)**

THIS CONCEPT IS THE KEY TO UNLOCKING THE REAL POTENTIAL, POWER, PRODUCTIVITY....AND ULTIMATELY THE SUCCESS OF ANY EMPLOYEE!

A WISE WORD...

"Man's biggest mistake is to believe that he is working for someone else"...Nashua Cavalier

Commentary;

Most of us will have to find a job...it's that simple. If we want to have money and take care of our families, it is one of the only ways to do it. A smaller few of us will have an idea for a product/service and decide to start our own enterprise. Suppose we started looking at our situation from the eyes of an employer. The truth of the matter is we are quick to see the paycheck we are getting now and not the bigger payoff we can get in the future. To be the best employee we can be (valued employee) and benefit the most from our employment we have to, as the quote suggest, stop making the mistake of just thinking that when we are employed we work for someone else. This is a crucial paradigm switch that if understood and applied will make you not only a valued employee in your current situation, but give you a life skill that is portable to any employment situation you may encounter. Let us be clear here, everyone is not cut out to be an employer. What we must learn is that while we may be working for someone else, we are truly working for ourselves. For this section we will look at the ideas as applying to both employee and employer. We do this so we can learn to create the circumstances whereby all benefit.

HOW DOES A BUSINESS CONTINUE TO OPERATE?

A simple way to look at owning a business is the same as it is for an individual on a budget: Make more money than you spend. The employer must know:

- His/her costs of doing business
- What employment resources are needed to produce the good/service
- How to utilize his "human resources" to realize a profit and stay in business
- How to increase the company's productivity to continue to employ workers and sustain the business.
- How to reduce turnover
- How to attract and keep good employees
- How to create an environment where the employees and the business can thrive

So let's discuss how the employee fits into this scenario.

WHAT EMPLOYERS NEED & WANT

- ❖ Employees that do the little things that save the company money
- ❖ Employees that understand that time is money
- ❖ Employees that seek to solve problems; without having to be told
- ❖ Employees that perform tasks that are "beyond" their job description
- ❖ Employees that understand the company's mission, values and place in the market
- ❖ Employees that understand that saving the company money translates to greater company profit and company growth
- ❖ Employees that are looking to help the company expand its product/service base
- ❖ Employees that understand the value of **CUSTOMER SERVICE!!!**
- ❖ Employees that are accountable
- ❖ Employees that are always improving their skills
- ❖ Employees that understand how they get paid
- ❖ Employees that understand why they work
- ❖ Employees that want to advance

❖ Employees that increase morale

IN THE END... EMPLOYERS DESIRE AND NEED EMPLOYEES WHO SEE THEIR WORK AS NOT JUST A JOB, BUT A REFLECTION OF THEIR CHARACTER. EMPLOYERS NEED EMPLOYEES WHO SEE THAT THEY MAKE A VALUABLE CONTRIBUTION TO THE WORKPLACE. MOST EMPLOYERS WANT TO SEE THEIR EMPLOYEES ADVANCE AND GROW IN THEIR COMPANIES. IT IS HOW ANY COMPANY BECOMES EVEN MORE PROFITABLE. THE WIN FOR THE EMPLOYEE IS THAT THIS DEDICATION TO BEING A "VALUABLE EMPLOYEE" MAKES THEM HARD TO REPLACE AND FOR THE EMPLOYEE MAKES HIS SKILLS TRANSFERABLE OUTSIDE HIS CURRENT EMPLOYMENT!!!

Discussion:

1. How do you rate yourself as you look at the list we reviewed?

_____

_____

_____

_____

2. Are you and your employer on the same page?

_____

_____

_____

_____

3. Does your employer know your name?

_____

_____

_____

_____

4. Do you contribute to making your employment environment the best it can be? (Morale)

_____

_____

_____

_____

5. Are you in it just for the money?

_____

_____

_____

_____

6. Do you see yourself growing with your current company?

_____

_____

_____

_____

7. Do you engage in gossip about others? About the company?

_____

_____

_____

_____

UNIT 4:

ENTREPRENUER COMPETENCY

COMMENTARY:

Starting, developing and maintaining your own business can be the most rewarding, fulfilling experience anyone can have. At the same time, it can be the hardest, challenging most frustrating experience anyone can have. There is a reason we are finishing the program with entrepreneurship. All business, whether working for someone, or working for yourself stems from entrepreneurship. The roots of being an entrepreneur are imbedded in the true wealth of this country. For this reason we will approach this section with an attitude of instilling in you not just the rudiments of becoming an entrepreneur, but the spirit, tenacity and "personality" of what makes up and drives the entrepreneurial mentality, because it is more than anything, a MENTALITY which can be learned and cultivated.

A WISE WORD.....

"Entrepreneurship is living a few years of your life like most people won't, so you can spend the rest of your life like most people can't"...author unknown.

This definition speaks to an attitude and a mindset....do you have it?

Discussion (Warm Up)

- What does this phrase say to you?

- Is it about money, or lifestyle?

- How do I acquire "entrepreneurial skills?

A WISE WORD: "Your talents and unique gifts will take you places you never dreamed you could go."

"We start with this wisdom because we believe that any great endeavor (business) has at its roots the gift, ability, aptitude or ingenuity of the person who starts the business. This is where your vision and power will come from when you are in doubt or want to give up. "There will be no greatness unless you endure to the end" (Rim Group 2013)

Entrepreneurship defined:

In <u>political economics</u>, **entrepreneurship** is a process of identifying and starting a business venture, sourcing and organizing the required resources and taking both the risks and rewards associated with the venture…wikopedia.org/wiki/entrepreneurship

As always we begin with a question. Was your understanding of being an entrepreneur the same as the definition describes?

This definition takes into account several elements. We will use these elements as the basis of our discussion

IDENTIFYING AND STARTING A BUSINESS VENTURE

The wisdom we quoted before speaks about a man's gift. In this instance we will use it to mean the unique thing that you bring to the table. It is fair to say that there is an idea, concept or service that only you may uniquely possess. This is crucially important. The world has enough hamburger stands, so why would you start another one unless it was so different that people would buy from you and you could make a profit? This said, let's list some concepts related to identifying what business venture you should start.

- Is there a viable market for your good or service?
- Is this a good time to start a business? (Do you have the time it takes to develop the business?)
- Do you have the necessary skills, training and back ground to deliver the good/service?
- Do you keep your day job?
- Do you understand how your business will make money?
- Are you just trading your job for another job?
- Do you handle money well?
- Do you have a business plan? (We will discuss later)

- Do you understand that there are legal steps you must take to start a business?
- Do you know the amount of capital you will need to start your business? (Start up cost)
- Do you have enough capital to survive until your business starts to make money (1 year)?

Truly asses your; strengths, weaknesses, opportunities and threats (SWOT ANALYSIS). This will be part of your business plan, but you need to know this before you even go into business. It is the **"what you are good at, what you are weak at, what your business can accomplish and what threats to achieving success for your business exists"**.

These are necessary questions you must ask yourself before you even consider opening the door to a new business. Once you have considered these questions and you feel that you can move on, you now must go through the necessary legal and business steps to have a legitimate business. When we say legitimate, we mean a business that can function practically and within the laws of the state you live in (government as well). This does not include or eliminate any regulatory issues you might face. Bottom line: you end the way you start. Our goal is to have an enterprise that is legally correct, and properly started. After all, your clients/customers will want and deserve this....

STEPS IN STARTING A BUSINESS (BEING LEGITIMATE)...THIS LIST IS NOT EXHUASTIVE AND WILL VARY FROM STATE TO STATE.

- Obtain a tax identification number (EIN) from the Internal Revenue Service (IRS) this can be done online or by phone.
- Incorporate your business in the state(s) you plan to do business. You will have to know the legal form your business will have (sole proprietor, partnership, LLC, C Corp) you should get advice on this. We suggest talking with a lawyer or business person who understands the different business types...THIS IS CRITICAL!!
- Make sure you register any trade names, brands, logos etc. with the state as well.
- For minority and women owned businesses you can seek to be a certified Minority Business Enterprise (MBE) or Women Owned Business Enterprise (WBE). You don't have to have these designations, but they are free to obtain and will give you the ability to do business with state and city governments and agencies. If you can't complete the application, there are firms that perform this service.
- Many cities and states require a bidder registration number to bid on their contracts. You may want to obtain this number.

We repeat, all states are different but, in most cases obtaining the information mentioned should allow you to do business in most states.

ACQUIRNG & ORGANIZING THE REQUIRED RESOURCES

It is critical to know what resources you will need in order to adequately run, and maintain your business!

If you followed the steps previously mentioned, your business can "legally" operate. To operate the business needs resources. As before, this list is not exhaustive but it will be a good guideline for you as you develop your business.

- You will need a business banking account.
- You will need to get an accountant or bookkeeper. There are software packages that are excellent and if you are good at using them, they are more than adequate. You need to keep records of your expenditures and revenues. You will also need well prepared financial statements (profit & loss and balance sheet at a minimum) your banks and investors will require this.
- You will need to prepare or have prepared taxes. You can't skip this, do it and sleep better.
- Have access to or retain a good lawyer. You don't have to pay a retainer, but you should be able to contact a lawyer in a timely manner. We live in a litigious world…. be prepared for the worst!

We mentioned in a previous step having a business plan. There is a saying that says "success doesn't just happen, it is intentional". A business plan should be your "road map", to guide you and keep you on track. We mention this step here because, if you have asked yourself the important questions we stated previously, there is a good chance the business you have chosen can be viable. A business plan will give you details, and provide an even clearer picture of what you will need in terms of resources, time and expertise in order for your business to have a real chance at being successful. Business planning will require you to look at your business critically and it will be an objective means by which you and others can ascertain the appropriateness of your ideas, and whether your business can attract capital. You need it to start and operate. Business plans can be elaborate and include many pages of information. That it is a decision you will have to make. There are plenty of resources to help you with this. We suggest taking the time to formulate your own business plan, and then have it looked at and reviewed by an objective party.

FINANCIAL RESOURCES:

All businesses need capital to start and continue to operate. The question of capital is one that all businesses face, from the largest to the smallest, whether start- up or an existing business. We discussed determining what your financial needs will be. Here we will talk about how and where we might obtain capital.

It's Not About
How Much
Money You
Make
It's How You
Save It!

Bank Financing: This type of financing will be the least expensive (financing cost), but the hardest to obtain. Banks require excellent credit, and they will want to know how you plan to repay the loan. They will require extensive documentation and will review your plans as to their viability. For a startup business it is safe to say bank financing will be difficult to obtain. If your credit is good you might seek the following loan options:

- ❖ Home equity loan
- ❖ Loan against a car title
- ❖ Loan for equipment you may need secured by the equipment
- ❖ An unsecured loan or note (must be extremely credit worthy)
- ❖ SBA (small business administration) this is a long process, but it is an option

KEY POINT: "QUID PRO QUO"...."SOMETHING FOR SOMETHING"

DEVELOP THE MIND SET THAT YOU MUST HAVE SOME "SKIN IN THE GAME"...WHAT WE MEAN IS, IF YOU WANT SOME ONE TO LOAN YOU MONEY OR INVEST IN YOUR ENTERPRISE, YOU MUST BE WILLING TO SUPPORT THE DEBT/INVESTMENT WITH SOMETHING OF VALUE, BE IT YOUR OWN INITIAL CAPITAL, COLLATERAL, EVEN YOUR "SWEAT EQUITY". THIS MIND SET IS CRITICAL TO ANYONE WHO CONSIDERS THEMSELVES AN ENTREPRENUER.....AT THE END OF THE DAY, THOSE THAT PROVIDE YOU CAPITAL ARE IN ESSENCE YOUR "PARTNER" THEY HAVE AN INTEREST IN YOU SUCCEEDING. YOU CAN NOT BE SERIOUS ABOUT BEING AN ENTREPRENUER IF YOU DON'T HAVE THIS MIND SET. ALL BUSINESS INVOLVES AN EXCHANGE....A SOMETHING FOR SOMETHING

OTHER SOURCES OF RAISING CAPITAL:

- Loans from friends/relatives
- Seek investors...you will have to be willing to give up a portion of your business (equity or percentage ownership)
- Be open to having a partner
- Online resources i.e. "crowd financing"

This list is not exhaustive, but it will give you a place to start. The bottom line is this:

YOU MUST HAVE ENOUGH CAPITAL AND RESOURCES TO SURVIVE (AT LEAST ONE YEAR). AS GREAT AS YOUR BUSINESS PLAN AND PRODUCT/ SERVICE MAY BE, IT WILL TAKE A WHILE FOR IT TO SUCCEED. IT IS ALSO IMPORTANT THAT YOUR BUSINESS HAS THE PROPER AMOUNT OF TIME TO "GET OFF THE GROUND". IT IS CRUCIAL THAT YOU UNDERSTAND THAT JUST BECAUSE YOU AREN'T MAKING MONEY IMMEDIATELY DOESN'T MEAN YOU WON'T SUCCEED. TO BE SUCCESSFUL AS AN ENTREPRENUER YOU MUST FIRST SURVIVE!!!

RISKS AND REWARDS:

A couple of quotes to get us started:

And the day came when the risk to remain tight in a bud was more painful than the risk it took to blossom. Anais Nin

If you don't risk anything you risk even more. Erica Jong

COMMENTARY:

Most of us can see rewards; most of us do not want to see risk. It is fact of life, but in business, it is the concept that you must embrace. Understand the simple fact that if you venture nothing you gain nothing. Understand that the great thing is the hardest thing to do sometimes. There are many success stories in life and in business. We must learn that risk and reward are not opposites, they work together. Understand that what you gain is always in direct proportion to what you are willing to give up getting it. A quote most often attributed to Peter Tosh says it all: **"EVERY BODY WANTS TO GO TO HEAVEN, BUT NOBODY WANTS TO DIE", HOW MUCH AND HOW BAD DO YOU WANT IT?**

SO WHAT ARE THE RISKS OF STARTING A BUSINESS?

- ✓ Business failure
- ✓ Legal and political
- ✓ Loss of money
- ✓ Loss of free time
- ✓ Stress to you, your family, your well being

1. What do you perceive as risk?

_____

_____

_____

_____

SO WHAT ARE THE REWARDS OF STARTING A BUSINESS?

* Financial security
* Creating a legacy for your family
* Using your creativity
* Self-actualization
* Control of your time (breakout session or handout to discuss…. "You can make more money, but you can't make more time")
* Being a positive resource to your community
* Creating employment for others
* Working now to not work later

How do risk and reward work together?

Every endeavor in life carries with it a mechanism by which we measure its success or failure-whether or not the gain is worth the effort. It is easy to look at a successful person or business and think they have it all without considering what it took for them to achieve the success. If we start out with an attitude that we want a business that is successful, worthwhile and creates the wealth we desire, we will accept the risk that goes with having that success. There is a world full of people who want something for nothing. There are few people who dare to dream and then work very hard to accomplish the dream. The marathon runner trades sweat and working out for crossing the finish line first. The farmer knows he must sow before he reaps. In either case, the outcome is not certain. In both cases, if they are ultimately successful they will have paid a price….all will not win or be successful in business. Most assuredly the ones that are successful carefully weighed out the risks and the rewards, saw them as companions and then GOT BUSY!!!! (RIM GROUP 2013)

THE FINAL WORD ON FINANCIAL COMPETENCY:

We live in age and time where we all see the bounty of a great society, founded on principals of hard work, and the opportunity to enjoy the freedom our country allows. The Declaration of Independence stated it for us: "that they are endowed by their creator with certain inalienable rights that among these are life, liberty and the pursuit of happiness." If you read any wise book at all, this is part of a wise plan. But even wise words, whether metaphor or catchphrase, will most often speak of circumstances with a condition that we must fulfill. The same is true of financial competency. The fruits and rewards are there for the taking; we must meet the condition to obtain the reward. There is no "magic bullet", nor is there a simple, easy way to get there. But there is a way to reach any of your goals, whether that is being a good employee/ employer, leaving your family with a legacy to build on, or not living in despair about your money and finances. The world speaks about money often. We all know the phrase "money is the root of all evil"….the truth is "it is the love of money that is the root of all evil". Our goal is not to be confused about the matter of money and finance. Our goal is to learn, understand and grow in the knowledge of financial matters. All will not be rich, but all have the ability to learn the concepts surrounding money and finance to better their life. It's that simple, and it is that true.

CONCLUDING WORD

"To prosper is to live life to the fullest, enjoying all the bounty that is ours by inheritance of this life. Embrace life, learn from it…grow with it…allow your life and purpose to inhabit the same space. Indulge your best and you will realize it." Leslie D. Reed, December 10, 2015

Printed in the United States
By Bookmasters